lala salama ⊞ sleep well

maembe ⊞ mangoes

mama ⊞ Mrs. or mother

matatu ⊞ taxi van

mjusi ⊞ lizard

nanasi ⊞ pineapple

ndege ⊞ bird

ndimu ⊞ limes

ndizi ⊞ bananas

ngiri ⊞ warthog

nguchiro ⊞ mongoose

nyani ⊞ baboon

nyati ⊞ buffalo

pembere ⊞ hyrax

rafiki ⊞ friend

safari ⊞ journey

simba ⊞ lion

soko ⊞ market

tafadhali ⊞ please

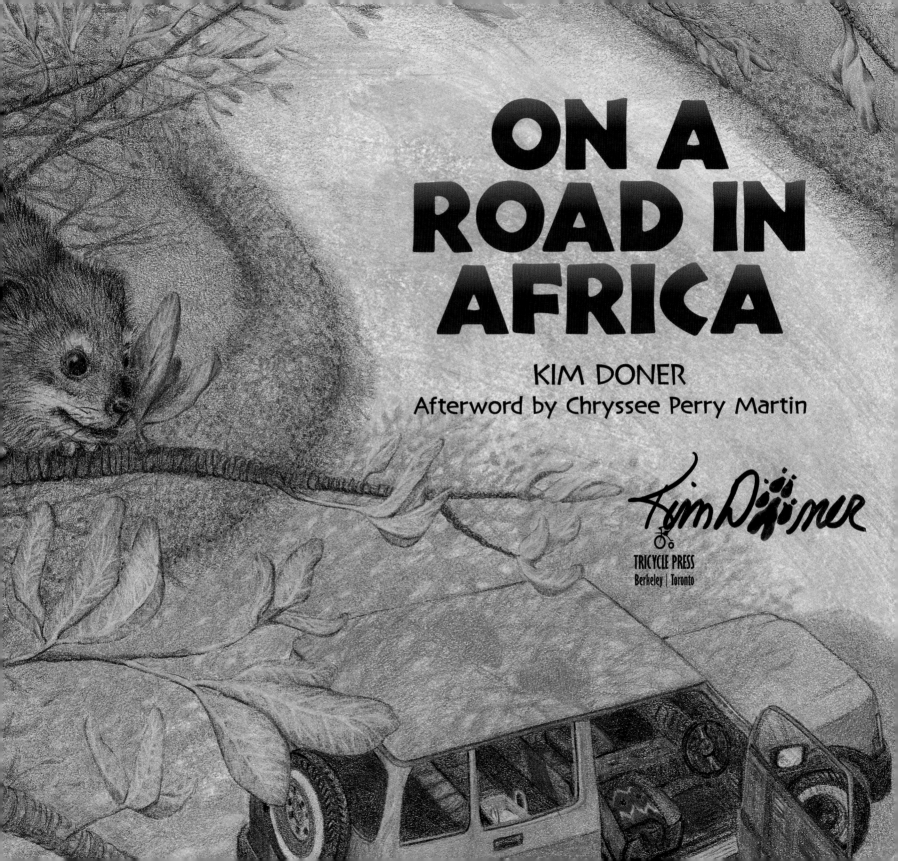

ON A ROAD IN AFRICA

KIM DONER

Afterword by Chryssee Perry Martin

TRICYCLE PRESS
Berkeley | Toronto

For Chryssee, of course! Also, with love and thanks to Linda Stilley and Farryl Stokes—dear friends who share friends with friends. —KD

To the members of the Animal Orphanage Team, who tend to all the needs of our four-legged friends, and to Esmond, who gives me tremendous support and encouragement. —CPM

Text and illustrations copyright © 2008 by Kim Doner

Tricycle Press
an imprint of Ten Speed Press
PO Box 7123
Berkeley, California 94707
www.tricyclepress.com

Design by Toni Tajima
Typeset in Asakire, Neuland, TheMix, Tsotsi
The illustrations in this book were rendered in markers, oil washes, pencil, and colored pencil.

Library of Congress Cataloging-in-Publication Data

Doner, Kim, 1955-
 On a road in Africa / written by Kim Doner with Chryssee Perry Martin ; illustrated by Kim Doner.
   p. cm.
 ISBN 978-1-58246-230-1
 1. Orphaned animals--Africa--Juvenile literature. I. Martin, Chryssee. II. Title.
 QL83.2.D66 2007
 636.08'32096762--dc22
                    2007018199
First Tricycle Press printing, 2008
Printed in Singapore

1 2 3 4 5 6 — 12 11 10 09 08

Baskets empty on the seat
Must be filled with things to eat.
Colored sisal, rough to feel,
Woven tightly, holds a meal.

On a road in Africa,
On a road in Africa.
Where you gonna go, Mama O, Mama O?
Where you gonna go, Mama O?

Countless feet carve dusty roads
Where people carry many loads.
They walk,
    they wait,
        they bike,
            they herd,
To say "Hello," they use the word **JAMBO!**

A weight is balanced on her head.
His shoulders make a moving bed.
Children watch, they learn, they try
And help their families to get by.

Where you gonna go, Mama O, Mama O?
                Where you gonna go, Mama O?

The **duka** door is open wide,
The owner welcomes all inside,
    "**Karibu**, Mama O! The order is ready
for your little ones. **Asante**."

    "Wonderful! And I thank you, too."

Matatus on the left and right
Packed with people, day and night.
Honking, revving, tires that squeal—
Voices from the beasts of steel.

On a road in Africa,
On a road in Africa.

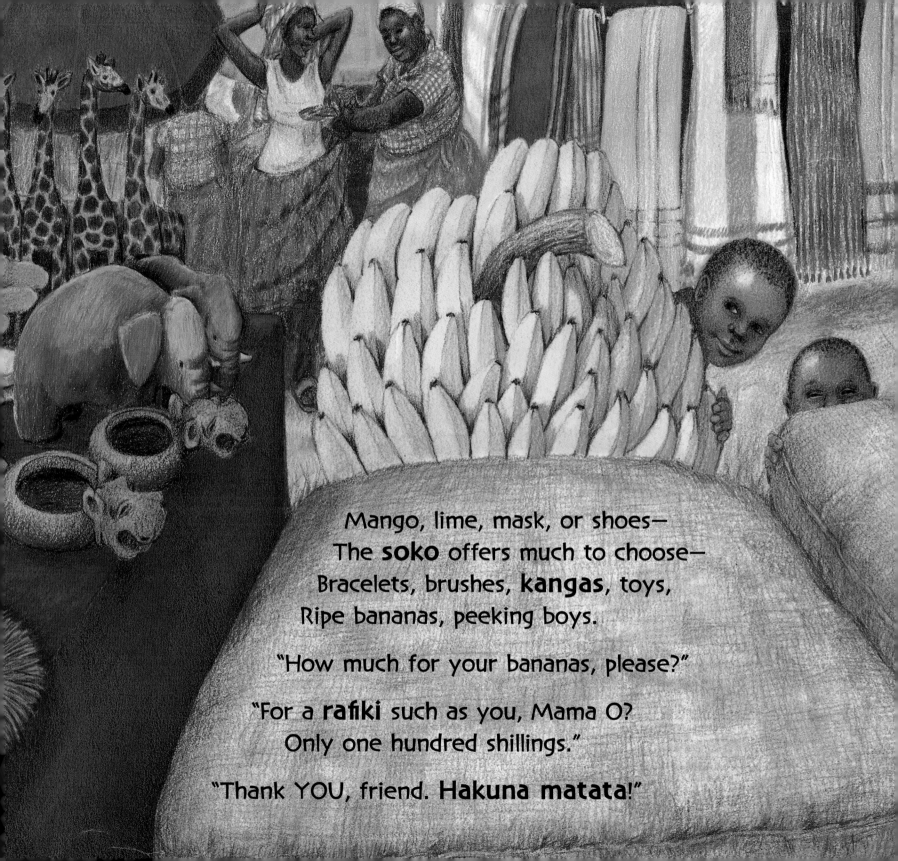

Mango, lime, mask, or shoes—
The **soko** offers much to choose—
Bracelets, brushes, **kangas**, toys,
Ripe bananas, peeking boys.

"How much for your bananas, please?"

"For a **rafiki** such as you, Mama O?
Only one hundred shillings."

"Thank YOU, friend. **Hakuna matata!**"

Children from the Banda School
Add their goodies to the pool.
In they pour a peanut rain,
Hear clunks from chunks of sugar cane.

Where you gonna go, Mama O, Mama O?
Where you gonna go, Mama O?

By the road may be a bunch
Who never think to bring their lunch.
It's YOUR food they want to snatch
And eat it all, then sit and scratch.

On a road in Africa,
On a road in Africa.

Volunteers can squeeze in back
Though each must hold a brimming sack.

This car is full, about to pop,
With only one more place to . . .

STOP!

"It is much safer up here,
Mr. Chameleon. Farewell!"

There's no time for long good-byes
With those baskets drawing flies.
Smelly gifts can spoil a ride—
Best if they are hung outside.

Where you gonna go, Mama O,
Mama O?
Where you gonna go, Mama O?

Hurry through the guarded gate.
It's supper time, do not be late.
Festus runs ahead to greet a
Hungry, eager, purring . . .

CHEETAH!

"**Jambo**, Tiva, here is some most very excellent meat for your dinner this evening."

For an orphaned buffalo,
Sugar cane to help him grow.
Then warthog care—inside and out.
Brush a bottom, feed a snout.

Peanuts meant for mouths and beaks
Are received with happy squeaks.
Monkeys help themselves to fruit,
Then the sneaks eat all their loot.

Stinky toys for each lion.
Using claws, they shred and try on
All the smells those baskets hold.
To us, it's poop—for them, it's gold.

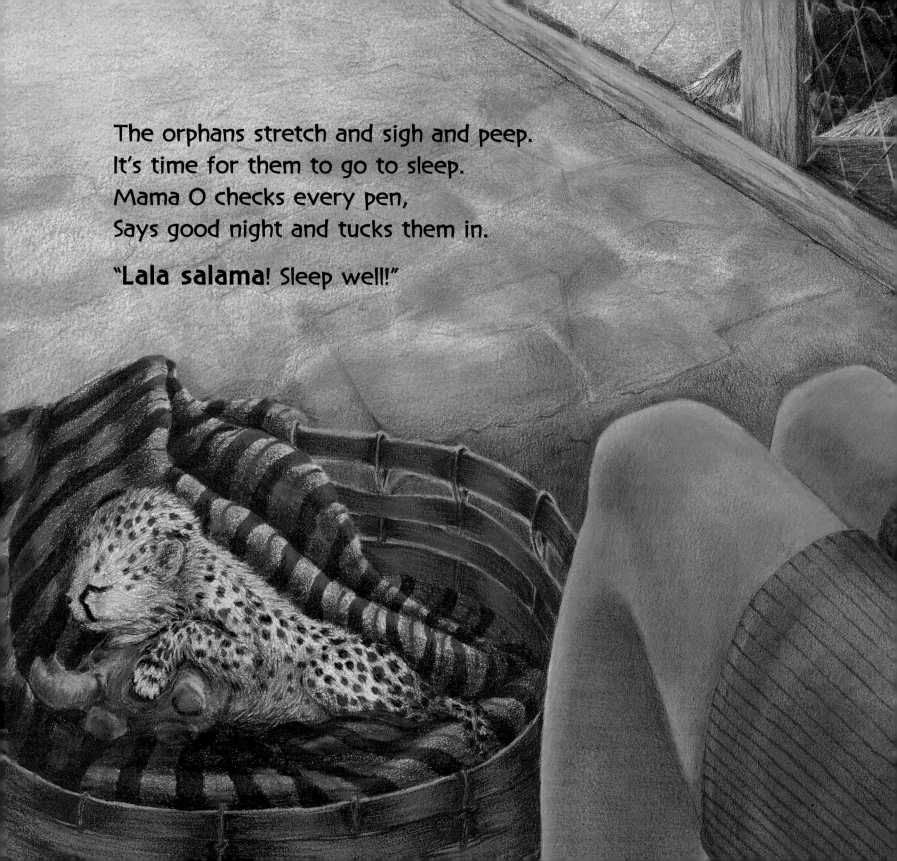

The orphans stretch and sigh and peep.
It's time for them to go to sleep.
Mama O checks every pen,
Says good night and tucks them in.

"**Lala salama!** Sleep well!"

Before you go, thank everyone,
Then, Mama O, your day is done.
Tomorrow comes with much to do.
Those empty baskets wait for you.

Where you gonna go, Mama O,
    Mama O?
Where you gonna go, Mama O?
    On a road in Africa,

        On a road

                to home.

Photo: Marcel Schoch

Perez Olindo, former director of the National Parks of Kenya, and Sharon Cheetah relax with Chryssee Perry Martin— Mama Orphanage.

Patricia and Patrick Warthog enjoy a basket of fresh-cut grass each day from Mama O.

Mama O handles every job, even dirty ones. Here, she gathers dung . . .

. . . packs it in a basket . . .

Photo: Marcel Schoch

Photo: Marcel Schoch

. . . and makes a toy that's a big hit with Charlie Lion!

Photo: Marcel Schoch

All photos on pages 42–43 by Kim Doner unless indicated.

THE REAL MAMA O

. . . is a ball of energy named Chryssee Perry Martin. Although she grew up in Tulsa, Oklahoma, she has lived in Nairobi, Kenya, for over thirty years and worked tirelessly as an honorary warden of the Kenya Wildlife Service in the Nairobi Animal Orphanage. Thanks to everyone who has joined her in these efforts, the Animal Orphanage has grown into a hands-on, playful place. New arrivals are doctored, fed, cuddled, and coddled. In fact, it's so comfy for the "residents" that many wild families, like warthogs and monkeys, have done their best to be adopted into the orphanage, too!

Chryssee has helped raise cheetahs, leopards, lions, duikers, mongooses, antelope, hyenas, and gazelles. When the orphanage calls in the middle of the night, she's ready to lend a hand. In 1991, the Kenya Wildlife Service celebrated her work by giving her a special title: Mama Orphanage. To share their love of African animals, Chryssee and her husband, Esmond, have written many books and articles about endangered rhinos and elephants. They travel worldwide to research what is happening to these animals and to educate people in ways to protect and help them.

A hyrax munches her daily carrots on Mama O's front porch.

Mama O rescued this lucky Jackson's chameleon from a busy street.

Every scene in this book has happened and happens still; every person exists and, this very moment, may be wrapping a snuggly blanket around a frightened baby baboon or heating milk for a tiny new cub. Kenyans, as well as people from all over the world, join to support their Animal Orphanage, where warthogs love to be brushed, cheetahs are petted daily, and lions enjoy rolling on smelly dung baskets.

I am a state and federally licensed wildlife rehabilitator and I take care of wildlife where I live in Oklahoma. When I met Chryssee, I was raising several baby squirrels and songbirds. We immediately became new best friends and visited for three hours straight. She told me her dream was to write a book for children about the animals at the orphanage. She invited me to come to Africa and see her world so we could create a book together. And here it is.

A portion of this book's sales will go directly to Mama O to help the orphanage. But what animal orphans *really* need is more Mama and Bwana O's.

Could that be you?

Where are YOU gonna go?

THE NAIROBI ANIMAL ORPHANAGE

Sometimes, in the wilds of Africa, baby animals lose their mothers. If a Kenya National Parks' Ranger finds an orphan, he sends it to the Animal Orphanage. The orphanage workers have saved the lives of many different kinds of wild animals, from hedgehogs (little creatures that look like porcupines but are only the size of a teacup fully grown) to leopards and lions.

Every young animal that comes to the orphanage is given a place to stay in the nursery, with a bed, play toys, and a person to bottle-feed and make them comfortable day and night. There is a signboard for each enclosure with the name of the animal, such as "Robert Buffalo," its close-up photo, and something about the animal's own personality. That way, everyone knows who's who and who likes what best.

When an animal such as a cheetah, warthog, or mongoose is old enough for visitors, it is put into an enclosure with everything that it needs to be happy. If the orphanage cannot release an animal after it grows up because it may not be able to take care of itself, the orphanage becomes its permanent home. Because all the orphans are used to people, they are very friendly. Some of the orphans even go for walks on leashes. Some come right up to their fences when called, hoping to be brushed or petted.

Samwel Otieno bottle-feeds hungry Sammy Cape Buffalo.

Lawrence Kasyoka often soothed Tiva Cheetah as a cub.

All the people who work in the orphanage enjoy taking care of the animals, and most of the animals have their special "people friends." The lions especially like Dave, who not only feeds them but also lets them snuggle up close. The baboons like Muigai, who lets them go through his pockets in search of peanuts. The leopard baby gets to chew on Marcel's jacket, and the mongooses play hide-and-seek with Festus.

On holidays, the orphans enjoy special treats. Valentine's Day features a competition for the prettiest valentine made for an orphan by a local child. Red hearts decorate all the trees and bushes in the orphanage. On Easter Sunday, the monkeys get colored hard-boiled eggs in Easter baskets. There are Christmas presents for all the orphans, including balls for the leopards, lions, and hyenas, bells for the parrots, and catnip for the Sokoke forest cats. One of the cheetahs wears a Santa Claus hat, and rangers give cookies to all the people who come to the orphanage. Visitors and animals love holidays!

Most important is that these animals are ambassadors for wildlife, showing visitors that wild animals are to be cherished.

Chryssee Perry Martin
Nairobi, 2007

Noah Bii invites Sharon Cheetah to be his Valentine.

Peter Achammer cuddled Talek Leopard when he was tiny.

Photo: Kim Doner

Festus Kioko and Rachel Mongoose celebrate Easter in style.

Growing leopards need comfort; Talek Leopard prefers Marcel's thumb.

Patrick Kivondo introduces Talek Leopard to baby Beatrice Mongoose.

Gerald Muigai brushes a content Patrick Warthog.

Marcel Schoch plays hide-and-seek with Marcel Hyena. Marcel the human never wins.

Dave Mascall unwinds with Romulus Lion Cub.

baboon ⊞ nyani
bananas ⊞ ndizi
basket ⊞ kikapu
bird ⊞ ndege
buffalo ⊞ nyati
cheetah ⊞ duma
danger ⊞ hatari
friend ⊞ rafiki
hello ⊞ jambo
hyena ⊞ fisi
hyrax ⊞ pembere
journey ⊞ safari
leopard ⊞ chui

limes ⊞ ndimu
lion ⊞ simba
lizard ⊞ mjusi